Copyright © 2024 Gavin O'Reilly.

All rights reserved.

Formatted by Zain Ul Hassan @ kdplancer

Cover Illustration by David Tobe Ezeoke

H-Block International

The Worldwide Reaction to The 1981 Irish Hunger Strike

by
Gavin O'Reilly

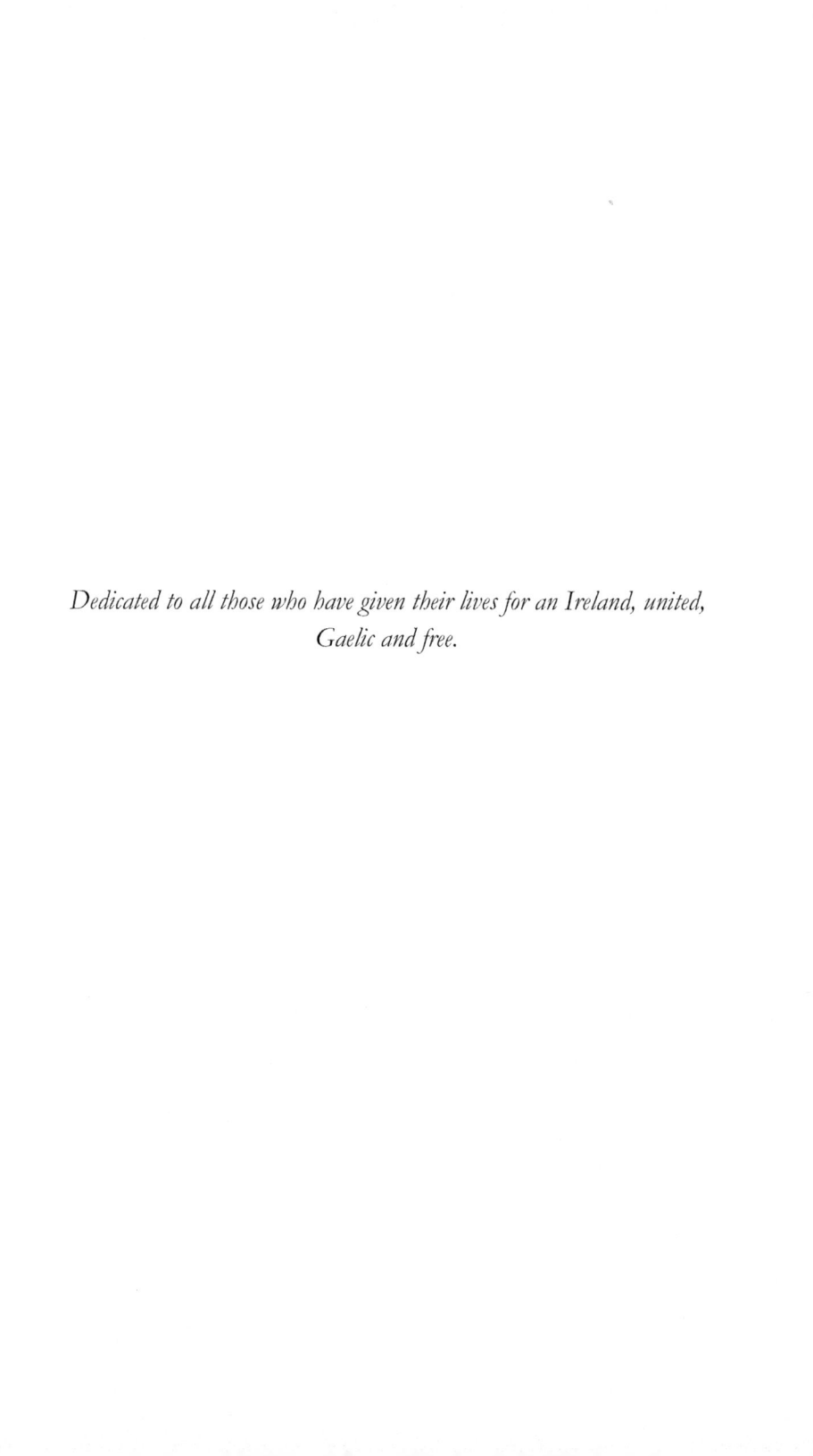

Dedicated to all those who have given their lives for an Ireland, united, Gaelic and free.

About the Author

Gavin O'Reilly is an accomplished writer in the realms of geopolitics and globalism. Since 2017, his work has appeared on *The Duran*, *Al-Masdar News*, *American Herald Tribune*, *MintPress News*, *Global Research*, *Popular Resistance*, *Blacklisted News*, *SouthFront*, *Off Guardian*, *Al Mayadeen*, *The Ron Paul Institute for Peace and Prosperity*, *21st Century Wire*, *ZeroHedge*, *Strategic Culture Foundation* and *Basira Press*, covering a wide range of topics from the wars in Syria and Yemen, to the Russian intervention in Ukraine, to the World Economic Forum's Great Reset agenda. He is also the author of the self-help book *Fear, Anger & Boxing - Mastering the Mind and Body*.

Table of Contents

Introduction 1

Background to the Hunger Strike 3

The Hunger Strikers 7
    Bobby Sands 7
    Francis Hughes 8
    Raymond McCreesh 9
    Patsy O'Hara 10
    Joe McDonnell 11
    Martin Hurson 12
    Kevin Lynch 12
    Kieran Doherty 13
    Thomas McElwee 14
    Michael Devine 15

Britain 17

United States 21

Australia 25

France 29

Vatican City 31

Canada 35

Cuba 37

Palestine 41

Iran 47

Aftermath of the Hunger Strike 53

Notes 59

Bibliography 67

Introduction

The 1981 hunger strike was one of the most seminal events of 20th century Irish history. Just like the 1916 Rising more than half a century beforehand, the hunger strike would also involve ordinary young Irishmen standing defiantly in the face of a political, economic and military power. Likewise, its subsequent emotional impact would shape politics in the north of Ireland for generations to come. What has generally been underlooked however, has been

how the 1981 hunger strike was viewed internationally at the time. From the United States to the Middle East, *H-Block International - The Worldwide Reaction to The 1981 Irish Hunger Strike* examines how the world viewed ten young Irishmen who refused to be labelled as criminals in the face of overwhelming odds.

Background to the Hunger Strike

On the 24th of April 1916, Easter Monday, Dublin would awake to the declaration in arms of the Republic, when the Irish Volunteers, led by Pádraig Pearse, seized the General Post Office and other key locations around the city. Fighting would last six days before eventually being quelled, with most of central Dublin left in ruins as a result.

Initially unpopular amongst the general public, opinion on the Rising would soon shift towards sympathy following the executions of the leaders, in particular Irish Citizen Army leader, James Connolly - gravely unwell at the time, and who had to be tied to a chair before being executed by a British firing squad.

In December 1918, the wave of nationalist and Republican sentiment that had emerged in the aftermath of the Rising would culminate in Sinn Féin recording a resounding success in that year's Irish general election. Refusing to take their seats in Westminster, the revolutionary Dáil Éireann council would be established on the 21st of January 1919 instead, with a guerilla war beginning against Britain on the same day.

Two years of conflict would follow before IRA leader Michael Collins, under threat of a *"terrible and immediate war"* by British Prime Minister David Lloyd George, would sign the Anglo-Irish surrender treaty, partitioning Ireland into a 26 county neo-colonial British puppet state to the south, and a British-ruled six county statelet with an inbuilt unionist majority to the northeast - the wider Ulster province having been subjected to a plantation of English and Scottish settlers in the 17th century and whose descendants still remained loyal to the British Crown.

A bloody year-long war would commence between former comrades as a result of the Treaty, with Collins himself becoming a high-profile casualty in August 1922. Once finished, the newly established southern Irish Free State would ultimately leave the nationalist community in the north of Ireland to fend for themselves, leading to decades of discrimination in terms of employment, housing, and education at the hands of the Stormont government.

Decades of simmering tensions related to these matters would eventually boil over in the 1960s. Following the civil rights marches in the United States and the student protests in France, a similar campaign would begin in the north of Ireland calling for equal rights for its nationalist population. The violent response of the unionist state towards these demonstrations however, would push many young nationalists towards militant Republicanism instead, in particular the Provisional IRA, which had formed in 1969 following a dispute within Republicanism on how to respond to the outbreak of violence.

This situation would ultimately culminate in Bloody Sunday in 1972, when British paratroopers opened fire on civil rights demonstrators in Derry, killing 13 people and leaving one man with fatal injuries he would later succumb to. The civil rights campaign effectively came to an end that day, and the north of Ireland, like the rest of the country half a century beforehand, would be swept by guerrilla warfare in the aftermath. A campaign that would soon reach Britain's shores, with the IRA beginning a bombing campaign against political, military and economic targets.

To combat this, Downing Street would adopt the strategy of Ulsterisation, Normalisation and Criminalisation. A three-pronged approach that would see the heavily-militarised RUC police force, alongside the locally-recruited Ulster Defence Regiment (UDR) of the British Army, given primacy in tackling the IRA (Ulsterisation), which in turn would allow the British government to portray the conflict as a provincial dispute (Normalisation), rather than a war on the British state by the IRA.

Thus, to complete this strategy, captured IRA Volunteers would be stripped of Special Category status, a de facto recognition by the British government that they were political prisoners, and would instead be legally regarded as common criminals once they entered the prison system (Criminalisation). A situation that would ultimately lead to the events of 1981.

In 1976, then-Secretary of State Merlyn Rees would sign a decree stripping Republican prisoners of political status. In response, Republican prisoners in the north of Ireland would engage in the blanket protest - a refusal to wear prison uniforms, using bed blankets to clothe themselves instead. Kieran Nugent, the first prisoner to be sentenced following the suspension of Special Category status, and thus the first blanket man, would famously declare that if the prison authorities wanted him to wear a uniform, they would have to nail it to his back.

The intransigence of the British state in dealing with the demands of Republican prisoners however, as well as the inhumane conditions they were subjected to, would see the situation escalate further, culminating in seven prisoners carrying out a 53-day hunger strike in late 1980. Following an appeal by Tomás Ó Fiaich, the then-Catholic Primate of Ireland, this hunger strike would be called off a week before Christmas that year, with a deal supposedly on the table that would have met the majority of the prisoners' demands.

When it soon became apparent that this would not occur however, the situation would take its most serious turn. On the 1st of March 1981, a hunger strike would once again begin in County Down's Long Kesh prison that would see ten young men - the youngest 23, the oldest 29 - starve to death rather than have their struggle labelled as criminal. The hunger strike, which would last until October that year, would have a seismic impact on Irish politics at the time, causing a landslide of support for militant Republicanism, just as the events of Bloody Sunday had done less than a decade earlier. Its impact would reach far beyond Ireland also, with people around the world astounded at the bravery of the young Irishmen making the ultimate sacrifice in the face of a centuries-old enemy. An impact that this book will explore.

The Hunger Strikers

Bobby Sands

The most well-known of the 1981 hunger strikers and the Commanding Officer of IRA prisoners in Long Kesh, Bobby Sands was born in Abbots Cross,[1] County Antrim on the 9th of March 1954, with his family later moving to the nearby Rathcoole estate while he was still a child.[2]

Though a rarity in the north of Ireland in that both nationalists and unionists co-existed peacefully in Rathcoole, rising tensions in the 1960s would ultimately foster division in the estate, with a teenage Bobby Sands finding himself ostracised[3] amongst former unionist friends amidst the deteriorating situation in the north of Ireland.

Leaving school at age 15 to pursue an apprenticeship as a coach builder, Sands would be on the receiving end of discrimination from unionist co-workers over his nationalist background, something he would initially ignore as he sought to develop his new career. An incident in 1971 however, when he was threatened at gunpoint by co-workers and forced to leave his job,[4] would prove to be a turning point. Amidst the ongoing violence in the north, Sands joined the ranks of the IRA.

A prison sentence would follow in 1972, when he was sentenced to several years for possession of firearms. Following his release in 1976, he would soon rejoin his comrades on active service. In October of that year, following the bombing of the Balmoral Furniture Company, chosen by the IRA for its economic value to the British, Sands would once again be

7

captured by Crown forces, this time receiving a much harsher 14-year sentence.

In late 1980, Bobby Sands assumed the role of Commanding Officer of IRA prisoners in Long Kesh, with the previous holder of the role, Brendan Hughes, having been on that year's hunger strike at the time. When the second hunger strike was planned, Sands would be at its forefront. On the 1st of March 1981, in protest against the removal of political status and criminalisation of Republican prisoners, Bobby Sands would begin the 1981 H-Block hunger strike, refusing food for 66 days until he passed away on the 5th of May aged 27, having begun a protest that would make history.

Francis Hughes

Francis Hughes was born on the 28th of February 1956 in Bellaghy, County Derry, to a family steeped in Republican tradition, with both his father and uncle having served roles with the IRA in the 1920s.[5]

Having initially joined the Official IRA - the opposing faction to the Provisional IRA which had emerged following the 1969 split, and which had dropped the long-standing Republican tradition of abstention from Leinster House and Stormont - Hughes would leave the organisation following its declaration of a ceasefire in 1972, and set up an independent Republican unit[6] in Bellaghy, one that would be absorbed into the structure of the Provisional IRA not long after. He would soon become one of that organisation's most effective Volunteers.

In 1977, Hughes was named as the most wanted man in the north of Ireland following a gun battle with the RUC that left two officers dead. He would remain on the run for almost a year before being captured following another shootout, this time with the SAS and which resulted in the death of one British soldier and the wounding of another.[7]

In February 1980, following a trial and conviction, Hughes would receive sentences totalling 83 years. Joining his comrades on the H-Blocks of Long Kesh, he would take part in the 1981 hunger strike a year later. Beginning on the 15th of March, two weeks after Bobby Sands had initially begun the strike, Hughes would pass away on the 12th of May, having gone 59 days without food.

Raymond McCreesh

Raymond McCreesh was born on the 25th of February 1957 in Camlough, County Armagh. Coming from a traditional Republican family, he would join Na Fianna Éireann, the IRA's youth wing, as a 16 year old,[8] before going on to become a member of the group's famed South Armagh Brigade.

In June 1976, aged 19, McCreesh would take part in an IRA operation that would involve the targeting of a British army observation post in Armagh. This would not go to plan however, when McCreesh and the other Volunteers were spotted by nearby paratroopers first, resulting in an ensuing gun battle and the subsequent capture of both McCreesh and two other IRA members.[9]

Receiving a 14-year sentence in 1977, McCreesh would join his comrades on the blanket protest, which by four years later, had escalated into a hunger strike in recognition of political status. Joining the hunger strike on the 22nd of March 1981, McCreesh passed away on the 21st of May, having gone 61 days without food.

Patsy O'Hara

Patsy O'Hara was born on the 11th of July 1957 in Bishop Street, County Derry. Joining Na Fianna Éireann as a 13-year old, he would be shot in the leg by a British soldier a year later in late 1971,[10] sustaining injuries that prevented him from attending the fateful civil rights march on Bloody Sunday, Having watched the events of the day from afar however, they would leave a lasting impact on the young O'Hara.

In October 1974, O'Hara was interned without trial in Long Kesh, and upon his release the following April, joined the Irish National Liberation Army (INLA)[11] - an armed Socialist Republican group that had split from the Official IRA the previous December in a dispute over how to deal with the ongoing violence in the north of Ireland; the Official IRA favouring a constitutional path, the INLA favouring a militant one.

Over the next several years, Patsy O'Hara would find himself in prison several times on both sides of the British-imposed border. Shortly after joining the INLA, he would be stopped at a checkpoint in Derry where the RUC planted explosives in his car in an attempt to frame him, resulting in six months on remand before he was acquitted.[12] The following year in 1976, he would spend another four months on remand on a weapons possession charge, one that was ultimately withdrawn by the judiciary.[13] Moving to the south of Ireland shortly afterwards, he would once again be arrested by Garda in Dublin and charged with holding an officer at gunpoint. Released on bail six weeks later, he would once again be acquitted in January 1978.[14]

Upon his return to Derry however, O'Hara would receive his most serious sentence. In January 1980, following his arrest and conviction for possession of a hand grenade,[15] he received eight years. Assuming the role of Commanding Officer of INLA prisoners in Long Kesh, he would join the ongoing blanket protest. On the 22nd of March 1981, he would then go on to join the hunger strike alongside Raymond McCreesh, passing away on the same day as him, the 21st of May, having gone 61 days without food.

Joe McDonnell

The oldest of the hunger strikers, though still a relatively young man at only 29, Joe McDonnell was born on the 14th of September 1951 on the Lower Falls Road in Belfast. Later marrying and moving to the Lenadoon estate, McDonnell would be arrested as part of Operation Demetrius in 1972,[16] a British army mass-arrest of suspected Republican sympathisers.

Spending several months as an internee on the Maidstone prison ship, then later Long Kesh, he would join the IRA's Belfast Brigade upon his release, with a further period of internment in Long Kesh following from 1973 until 1974.[17] McDonnell's most serious imprisonment would come in 1976, when alongside his comrade Bobby Sands, he took part in an IRA operation targeting the Balmoral Furniture Company as part of the organisation's campaign to strike at economic targets. Captured shortly afterwards, both men would receive 14-year prison sentences for possession of a firearm.

Serving as an IRA prisoner in Long Kesh, he would take part in the blanket protest, resulting in prison authorities banning him from visits with his wife and two young children, a situation that would last until he joined the hunger strike on the 8th of May 1981[18] and had subsequently entered his final days. On the 8th of

July, Joe McDonnell passed away, having gone 61 days without food.

Martin Hurson

Martin Hurson was born on the 13th of September 1956 in the village of Cappagh, County Tyrone, a hotbed of Republican activity that the young Martin would soon find himself involved in.

In November 1976, aged only 20, Hurson was arrested with six other men in relation to the planting of explosives by the IRA, and subjected to brutal torture by his RUC captors, forcing the young Tyrone man to sign a confession in order to alleviate the brutality.[19] Despite there being no forensic evidence to link Hurson or the other six men to the explosives, the forced confessions were enough to have him convicted a year later[20] on a number of charges relating to IRA membership, possession of explosives, and conspiracy to kill members of the security services. Hurson received sentences varying in length from twenty, fifteen and five years.[21]

Having been remanded in Long Kesh following his initial charging, Hurson would join his comrades on the blanket protest, before ultimately going on to join the hunger strike on the 29th of May 1981. Losing the ability to hold water down around the 40 day mark, his condition would deteriorate rapidly and he would pass away on the 13th of July, having gone 46 days without food.

Kevin Lynch

Kevin Lynch was born in the villlage of Park, County Derry on the 25th of May 1956. Joining Na Fianna Éireann as a teenager, he would then move onto the Official IRA.[22] He would leave that organisation following its declaration of a ceasefire in 1972 however, before going on to join the ranks of the INLA several years later.[23]

In November 1976, following an ambush on a RUC patrol in nearby Dungiven, resulting in the wounding of one officer, authorities sought to round up all local suspected INLA members. In early December, Lynch was arrested with three other men and charged with stealing legally-held firearms, taking part in a punishment shooting, and conspiring to disarm members of the security services in a bid to procure weapons for the INLA.[24]

Following a year on remand in Belfast's Crumlin Road Gaol, Lynch would be convicted of all charges, sentenced to ten years, and sent to the H-Blocks of Long Kesh. Joining the ongoing blanket protest at the time, he would then become the second INLA Volunteer to join the 1981 hunger strike after Patsy O'Hara. Beginning on the 23rd of May, Lynch would pass away on the 1st of August, having gone 71 days without food.

Kieran Doherty

Kieran Doherty was born on the 16th of October 1955 in Andersonstown, Belfast. Taking a keen interest in GAA during his youth,[25] Doherty would also go on to join Na Fianna Éireann in 1971 aged 16,[26] with the ongoing violence in six counties being a key factor in his decision.

Soon proving himself to be a committed and disciplined young Republican, attention from the British would quickly follow. In February 1973, Doherty would be interned without trial in Long Kesh, not being released until November 1975 after an almost three year period.[27] Undeterred and unwavering, he would report back to the IRA upon his release, where he would soon receive his most serious sentence.

In August 1976, as part of a five-man IRA unit, Doherty was tasked with the transportation of a bomb. Using a van to move the device through Belfast, the men would be spotted by an RUC patrol who subsequently gave chase.[28] Exiting the vehicle and commandeering a nearby car, Doherty would be arrested a mile and a half later. Despite there being no forensic evidence to link him to the van, or eyewitness accounts that would have seen him leaving it,[29] Doherty was subsequently convicted and sentenced to a total of 22 years, with 18 for possession of explosives and firearms, and 4 for the commandeering of the car.[30]

Joining his comrades in the H-Blocks, he would begin to refuse food on the 22nd of May 1981, passing away on the 2nd of August, a 73 day period that was the longest out of any of the 1981 hunger strikers.

Thomas McElwee

Thomas McElwee was born on the 30th of November 1957 in Bellaghy, Derry. Similar to other hunger strikers, he would also join Na Fianna Éireann as a youngster, before going on to join the independent Republican unit led by his cousin Francis Hughes, ultimately becoming an IRA member once said unit was incorporated into the structures of that organisation.[31]

In October 1976, while transporting explosives to be used against economic targets in the town of Ballymena, a premature explosion would result in McElwee losing his right eye. After a seven week stay in hospital under armed guard, McElwee would be charged with possession of explosives, and the murder of of a young woman who died tragically when one of the planted bombs had detonated before she had a chance to evacuate the targeted location, with McElwee's unit having rung in a short-notice warning to the emergency services beforehand in order to clear civilians - an IRA protocol.[32]

Convicted of both charges, the murder conviction would later be downgraded to manslaughter following an appeal, however a twenty year sentence still remained.

Going on the blanket with the rest of his comrades, McElwee would become the ninth hunger striker on the 8th of June 1981, passing away exactly two months later on the 8th of August after 62 days without food. At 23 years old, he was the joint youngest hunger striker alongside Patsy O'Hara, McElwee being the younger of the two by four months.

Michael Devine

Michael "Mickey" Devine was born on the 26th of May 1954 in the Springhill Camp, a rundown former US military base in Derry, used to house the city's nationalist population since the end of the second World War. A prime example of the discrimination that nationalists faced in being housed by the Stormont regime, the camp would eventually be declared not fit for purpose and young Mickey and his family would be moved to the Creggan estate in 1960.[33] This is where events would occur that would have a formative effect on the young Derry man and the path he would ultimately choose in life.

In 1968, Derry, with a majority nationalist population, would become a flashpoint in the violence that was beginning to sweep the six counties. The first civil rights demonstration would take place in the city on the 5th of October, resulting in hundreds of protesters being brutalised by the RUC. Devine, only fourteen at the time, would later recall that at the start of that fateful day he didn't even know there was a protest taking place, but having seen its events on the television, would be throwing rocks at the RUC by the end of it.[34]

Going to join the Labour Party and the Young Socialists, Devine would become actively involved in the ongoing civil rights campaign. The subsequent events of Bloody Sunday would evoke a more militant side in the young Devine however, and he would then go on to join the Official IRA. Again, having quickly become aware of the reformist path that that organisation was on, Devine would ultimately go on to become a founding member of the INLA.[35]

In September 1976, in a bid to obtain weapons for the fledgling organisation, Devine and a number of other INLA members would take part in a raid on a private armoury in Donegal, acquiring a number of rifles and shotguns, and 3,000 rounds of ammunition. This would be an operation that would prove to be ill-fated however, when Devine was arrested later that day and charged with theft and possession of firearms.[36] Remanded in Crumlin Road for nine months, Devine would be convicted of all charges in June 1977 and sent to Long Kesh, where he would immediately join the blanket protest.

On the 22nd of June 1981, Devine would join the hunger strike, passing away 60 days later on the 20th of August, aged 27. The last of the hunger strikers to die, in a protest of which the impact was felt not just in Ireland, but throughout the world. An impact that this book will now examine.

Britain

Ironically, the country that had ultimately caused the 1981 hunger strike, would also have a high Irish population, in particular since the 19th century.

For a seven year period between 1845 and 1852, the outbreak of blight in Europe would have a particularly devastating effect on Ireland, where potatoes would form a staple part of the diet. Despite Ireland being ruled directly by Westminster as a result of the 1801 Acts of Union however, Downing Street's reliance on laissez-faire capitalism would see little in the way of aid coming Ireland's way at the time, with the British establishment pinning their hopes on free market economics resolving the crisis, rather than a direct intervention by the state - a stance that would exacerbate the situation in a most lethal fashion.

Indeed, Charles Trevelyan, Assistant Secretary to the Treasury and the British government official tasked with administering emergency aid to Ireland during this period, and who saw the blight as a divine punishment of the Irish,[37] would recount in private correspondence with Poor Law Commissioner Edward Twistleton that the selling of land by Irish farmers amidst the crisis would ultimately prove beneficial to English capital, who would then be able to purchase the land at a reduced price.

Effectively an act of genocide against the Irish people through mass-starvation, *An Gorta Mór* (The Great Hunger) would ultimately result in the deaths of one million[38] Irish people through disease and starvation, and the further forced emigration of one million[39] more, particularly to the United States, and also

17

to Britain, where, having settled in cities like Liverpool, London and Manchester, they would be used as cheap labour by English industrialists. The establishment of these Irish communities in Britain, would also play a key impact more than a century later in the international reaction to the 1981 H-Block hunger strike.

Under the rule of Margaret Thatcher's Tory government, the British media's reaction to the hunger strike was one of universal condemnation. The Irish community in Britain were undeterred however, and held numerous events in support of the hunger strikers, with some of the earliest occurring in London. On the 7th of March 1981, six days after the hunger strike had begun, Sinn Féin's London branch defied a temporary ban on all street marches in the city to host a public meeting on the strike at Kilburn Square.[40] Several weeks later, a major propaganda coup would be scored at the inaugural London Marathon. Finished in a dead heat by the joint winners, Dick Beardsley of the United States and the Norwegian Inge Simonsen, who famously crossed the finish line holding hands, two demonstrators would enter the marathon path close to its finish, holding aloft a banner with *"Victory to the Irish Hunger Strikers"* emblazoned across it. Though quickly ushered away by nearby police, their act of protest would be viewed by millions around the world.

As the hunger strike commenced, further demonstrations would be held throughout Britain in support. On the 9th of April, Bobby Sands was elected as an MP, on the traditional Republican basis of abstaining from taking seats in Stormont or Westminster. The following day, Sinn Féin held a packed public meeting in London's Conway Hall,[41] and a street meeting in Brixton,[42] where riots would break out on the same day as a result of tensions between the area's black community and the London

Metropolitan Police. Brixton is also notable for its namesake prison, where IRA prisoners were held at the time.

Indeed, just as street demonstrations would continue in the weeks that the hunger strike progressed, the IRA itself would carry out acts in support. On the 26th of April, IRA prisoners in London's Wormwood Scrubs, would scale the building's roof and stage an overnight protest in support of the hunger strike.[43] This would come only a week after Sinn Féin's Easter commemoration in London, which attracted several hundred participants.[44] On the 4th of May, the eve of Bobby Sands' death, a similar demonstration would take place in Worcestershire's Long Lartin prison, where five IRA prisoners would scale the rooftop and once again hold aloft banners in support of the hunger strike.[45]

The ensuing deaths of the ten hunger strikers and their subsequent emotional impact, would result in Margaret Thatcher becoming a particular figure of hate within Irish Republicanism, and this would prove to be a key factor in the IRA's decision making in the aftermath.

On the 12th of October 1984, a bomb would rip through the Grand Hotel in the coastal town of Brighton, resulting in five deaths. The hotel was hosting the annual Conservative Party conference at the time, and Margaret Thatcher and her Cabinet Ministers were present, narrowly escaping being killed in the blast.

The IRA had come within a whisker of carrying out their most spectacular coup and wiping out the entire British government, something that was ominously echoed in their now famous statement claiming responsibility for the attack, declaring *"Today we were unlucky, but remember, we only have to be lucky once. You will have to be lucky always"*. Despite taking place three years after the event, it would perhaps be the most significant response to the 1981 hunger strike in Britain.

United States

Similar to Britain, the United States would also experience a massive influx of Irish immigrants in the 19th century as a result of The Great Hunger. Settling primarily along the east coast in states like Massachusetts, Pennsylvania and New York (where they would play a key role in the construction of the city's famous skyline), the Irish diaspora would form tight-knit communities in the US, keeping their culture and traditions alive in spite of being forced from their homeland. Indeed, it would be this community spirit amongst Irish-Americans that would play a prominent role in the international response to the H-Block hunger strike more than a century later.

In 1969, Michael Flannery, a Tipperary-born immigrant to the US who had previously fought with the IRA in the 1920s, would establish the Irish Northern Aid Committee, more commonly known as NORAID, in response to the outbreak of violence in the north of Ireland. Intended as a support network for the families of Republican prisoners, NORAID would host regular formal dinner events, as well as fundraising in Irish-American bars, in order to achieve this aim. It would also publish a newsletter, known as *The Irish People*, that kept the diaspora up to date on the situation back home in Ireland.

Another more direct role would also be taken amongst members of the Irish-American community in their support for militant Republicanism. Amidst the outbreak of violence in the north, George Harrison, an Irish immigrant to New York, who like Flannery had also been a member of the IRA, and who still maintained close ties to Ireland, would establish a key gun-running network to the Provisional IRA at the beginning of the

70s. Twenty years previously, Harrison would also be involved in the smuggling of arms into Ireland as part of the IRA's Border campaign, a smaller scale guerrilla campaign to end British rule in the north. Harrison's latter gun-running operation however, would take place on a far more significant level, providing the bulk[46] of the IRA's weaponry throughout the 70s up until his trial, alongside Flannery, in a 1981 arms smuggling case in New York; one which would end in acquittal for all defendants owing to allegations of CIA involvement[47] in the prosecution. By this stage, the IRA had already established other international gun-running networks to continue its campaign. The ongoing support of the Irish-American community for Republicanism however, would play a crucial role in the international response to that year's hunger strike.

At the outset of the hunger strike, regular solidarity demos[48] would be held in cities like New York, Boston and Chicago (all possessing a significant Irish-American population), and they would grow in magnitude as the strike progressed. Indeed, such was the impact of the hunger strike, that the US political establishment would also become involved. Mario Biaggi, an outspoken Congressman from New York, and member of the Irish National Caucus lobby group, had become one of the most vocal supporters of Irish reunification since the outbreak of violence in the north. Having previously appealed to the UN to mediate in the 1980 hunger strike,[49] Biaggi would become the most prominent advocate of the follow up 1981 strike in the US political sphere, declaring to Congress in the wake of Bobby Sands' death that he hoped that the British government would *"suffer the glare of a much deserved negative world reaction"*.[50] Bernie Sanders, future US Presidential nominee and then mayor of Burlington, Vermont, would write a strongly worded letter to the government of Margaret Thatcher,[51] condemning the treatment of Republican prisoners in the north of Ireland, and the White House, under the administration of Ronald Reagan, an Irish-American yet Thatcher's strongest ally, would issue a statement upon the death of Bobby Sands, expressing its concern and regret at the situation in Ireland.[52]

Following Sands' death, New York would become the epicentre of the US response to the hunger strike. The city's Archbishop, Cardinal Terence Cooke, the son of Irish immigrants, would hold a mass[53] in Manhattan's St.Patrick's Cathedral, calling for peace and reconciliation in the north of Ireland. The International Longshoremen's association, a New York-based trade union representing dock workers, announced a 24-hour boycott[54] of British ships to coincide with Sands' funeral on the 7th of May, and protests would continue outside the city's British Diplomatic Mission, alongside similar protests in Chicago[55] and San Francisco.[56]

In order to save face, the then-British Prince, Charles Windsor was sent on a publicity tour of the US in June, at which stage four of the hunger strikers had died. Attending a reception at New York's Lincoln Centre alongside First Lady Nancy Reagan, he would be met by a crowd of 20,000 protesters, including amongst them the brothers of Bobby Sands and Raymond McCreesh, and the sisters of Patsy O'Hara and Joe McDonnell.[57] Later that night he would attend the Royal Ballet in the city's Metropolitan Opera House, where he would be heckled by four Republican sympathisers who had gained entry to the event before being swiftly removed by security.[58] Later bemoaning his experience to then-mayor of New York Ed Koch, he would be advised by the city official, who had known Irish sympathies, to *"get out of Ireland"*. A planned follow up visit to the US by Princess Margaret was subsequently cancelled.[59]

H-BLOCK INTERNATIONAL

In New Jersey, the state assembly passed a motion extending its condolences to the family of Bobby Sands[60] and condemning the British government. Likewise in Massachusetts, the Senate passed a similar motion extending their condolences to the Sands family, and declaring that Sands had *"once again demonstrated to the world that true Irish patriots desire Ireland's freedom encompassed in one nation"*.[61]

Indeed, even as the years passed following the hunger strike, its impact on the US was still acknowledged. In May 1997, 16 years after the death of Bobby Sands, a memorial cross was erected in Hartford, Connecticut - another state with a strong Irish connection - commemorating the hunger strike. Listing the names of the names of the ten men who died in 1981, it would also include the names of Michael Gaughan and Frank Stagg, two IRA Volunteers who died on hunger strike in British prisons in 1974 and 1976 respectively. Commissioned by NORAID and local Irish-Americans, and the only monument of its kind in the United States, the Bobby Sands Memorial Cross serves as a permanent reminder of the impact that ten young Irishmen would have on the American public in 1981.

Australia

Like Britain and the United States, Australia also possesses a population of which a significant percentage can claim Irish heritage. Unlike Britain and the US however, the origins of the Irish in Australia lie not primarily in The Great Hunger, as Australia would not have been a feasible location for most of the impoverished Irish to travel to at the time, but rather in Irish revolutionary activity that had taken place several decades beforehand.

In 1798, rebellion would sweep Ireland, when the Society of United Irishmen staged an uprising against British rule, receiving the assistance of a French military intervention in doing so, with Paris being involved in the Revolutionary Wars against Britain at the time and thus, regarding London as a common enemy. Despite this extensive French support, the failure of their forces to coordinate effectively with the Irish rebels would ultimately result in the insurrection being defeated after several months. The possibility that Britain could have suffered a severe military and political defeat at the hands of a more organised French campaign in Ireland however, was not lost on Downing Street, and stringent measures were put in place to curb the influence of Republicanism. Those convicted of taking part in revolutionary activity at the time were sentenced to exile in British penal colonies in what is now modern-day Australia.

Indeed, this would be the subject of *Back Home in Derry*, a song written by Bobby Sands while imprisoned in Long Kesh, recounting the experience of an Irish rebel exiled to Van Diemen's Land (modern-day Tasmania) in the aftermath of the 1803 Rebellion - a smaller scale follow up to the 1798 rebellion focused mainly in Dublin, and which resulted in the capture and execution of its leader, Robert Emmett, by the British.

The revolutionary ideals of the Irish exiles would seemingly pass down the generations in Australia however, as almost two centuries later, Oceania would also engage in displays of solidarity with ten young Irishmen thousands of miles away, who refused to be labelled as criminals.

The Irish National Association of Australasia (INA), a group set up by Irish immigrants in Sydney in 1915 in order to keep Irish culture and tradition alive amongst the diaspora, would be at the forefront of events highlighting the ongoing hunger strike in the north of Ireland when it began in 1981. Joining them would be Australian Aid for Ireland, a newly formed NORAID-style organisation that, like its US counterpart, would also seek to raise funds for the dependents of Irish political prisoners, and awareness of the ongoing situation in Ireland amongst the Australian public.

In another similar fashion to the US, events in Australia related to the hunger strike would also grow in magnitude as the strike progressed.

On the 1st of May 1981, as Bobby Sands entered his final days, a candlelit vigil in Sydney would attract over 200 supporters.[62] Following Sands' subsequent death on the 5th of May, a crowd of over 5,000 demonstrators would gather at the INA's headquarters in Sydney before marching to the city's British Consulate in protest.[63] Sydney's St. Patrick's Cathedral, in a similar fashion to its New York namesake, would also hold a Mass[64] calling for peace in reconciliation in the north of Ireland, attracting over 2,000 mourners, as would a similar mass in

Melbourne's identically named St. Patrick's Cathedral on the same day.[65]

As the weeks passed and more of the hunger strikers died, Australian displays of solidarity would continue. In June, at which stage four prisoners had died, a British ship, *The Cape Horn*, would be prevented from leaving Port Kembla in New South Wales,[66] as a result of a 48-hour refusal by the Waterside Workers' Federation to load its British bound cargo of grain. The most serious show of solidarity in Australia however, would come in August, following the death of Thomas McElwee.

On the 9th of August, one day after McElwee had died, Eamon "Ned" O'Connor, an Irish immigrant from Tullamore, County Offaly, announced to a crowd that had gathered in protest at the British Consulate in Sydney that he would begin a hunger strike in solidarity with Republican prisoners in the H-Blocks, and would only cease once the Australian government had called on Britain to formally recognise them as political prisoners. Carrying out this hunger strike in the city's INA headquarters, O'Connor would go 39 days without food,[67] ending his fast on the 17th of September (at which stage, Michael Devine, the last of the hunger strikers to die, had already passed away) after a message from the IRA leadership in Ireland was relayed to him, specifically requesting him to do so.[68]

Though the Irish hunger strike would subsequently come to an end, its memory would still remain in the Australian conscious decades later. In 1994, the INA placed a plaque commemorating the hunger strike on the 1798 monument in Sydney's Waverley Cemetery. The structure of the original monument incorporates the grave of Michael Dwyer, a leading member of the 1798 rebellion who died in exile in Australia. In 2015, a street in Brisbane would also be named after Bobby Sands by Irish-born local councillor Victor Attwood,[69] another lasting reminder of the impact that ten young Irishmen would have across the globe in 1981.

France

As mentioned in the previous chapter, the revolutionary history of Ireland shares an almost spiritual interconnectedness with that of France.

Both Celtic nations, the French Revolution of the late 18th century would play a hugely influential role in the rise of Republicanism in Ireland, and the subsequent Irish rebellions of 1798 and 1803. As well as the aforementioned French military intervention in 1798, a much larger scale expedition to Ireland, involving 15,000 French troops, had been planned two years previously in December 1796. Though ultimately scuppered by atrocious weather conditions, had this significant military force landed in Ireland unimpeded, it is likely that both Irish and wider European history would have taken a radically different course. Indeed, Wolfe Tone himself would later call it England's greatest escape since the Spanish Armada.

Likewise, the student protests that swept France in the Summer of 1968, as well as the civil rights demonstrations occurring in the US at the same time, would also serve as a continuing inspiration to the ongoing civil rights campaign that had begun in the north of Ireland in 1966. In turn, this would lead to a violent state response by Britain, culminating in the rise of the IRA and INLA, and decades of guerrilla warfare against the British occupation. Again, this in turn would lead to the situation where Britain employed a policy of criminalisation against Republican prisoners, which would ultimately lead to the 1981 hunger strike.

As such, the impact of the hunger strike would be felt in France, and upon the death of Bobby Sands, thousands would take to the streets of Paris in support of the demands of the Irish prisoners, gathering behind a huge portrait of Sands to chants of *"The IRA will conquer"*.[70] In Toulouse, a warehouse owned by British tyre firm Dunlop would be targeted in a bomb attack by French activists, with the slogan *"English power kills"* found sprayed on a nearby wall.[71]

In the cities of Nantes, Saint-Étienne and Le Mans, the small rural town of Vierzon, and the Parisian suburb of Saint-Denis, a number of streets would be named after Bobby Sands. A street in Lyon would be named after Patsy O'Hara also. Decades later, the impact of the 1981 Irish hunger strike on the Gallic nation would still linger on.

In 2013, a dispute arose when, following the death of Margaret Thatcher, a proposal was put forward to name a street in Paris after the former British Prime Minister.[72] Countering the motion, a councillor proposed that the street be named after Bobby Sands instead, which would have led to two Parisian streets being named after the Belfast man.

Though neither motion was ultimately successful, the debate once again showed the impact that the 1981 Irish hunger strike had had abroad, this time in France.

Vatican City

Although Irish Republicanism has traditionally been regarded as a secular ideology, a religious element has been present throughout much of the struggle for independence from British rule.

By the late 16th century, English rule in Ireland was concentrated in a south-eastern Dublin-centred area known as *The Pale*, with the vast majority of the country still remaining under the control of Gaelic Chieftains, whose influence was felt most strongly in the northern province of Ulster.

Attempts by England to further extend its rule throughout Ireland, and a number of rebellions by Irish leaders against such measures, would ultimately culminate in the Nine Years War from 1594 to 1603, between the forces of Earl of Tyrone Hugh O'Neill and the English Crown. The eventual defeat of Ulsterman O'Neill, and his subsequent exile and death in Spain, would mark the end of Gaelic rule in Ireland, and would bring the entire country under English control, with London soon seeking to rubber stamp its authority on the province that had been most belligerent towards its advances.

At the beginning of the 17th century, thousands of English and Scottish settlers were moved into Ulster, being accommodated on lands confiscated from the native Irish by the English Crown. With the English settlers predominantly being Anglican, and the Scottish predominantly being Presbyterian, this would inevitably add a religious element to the tensions that would arise with the predominantly Catholic Irish.

In 1641, this would lead to a large-scale uprising against British rule in Ireland, resulting in much of the country once again coming under the control of Irish Catholics. Establishing a Confederation which was composed of a strategic alliance with supporters of King Charles I, engaged in the English Civil War at the time, this arrangement would last until the defeat and execution of Charles in 1649. A genocidal four year campaign to reconquer Ireland, led by Oliver Cromwell, would begin immediately afterwards, leading to the introduction of penal laws that would prevent Catholics from entering Parliament, voting, or owning land - a legal situation that remained in place until the early 19th century.

As such, when Ireland was partitioned in 1922, the majority of unionists and loyalists came from a Protestant background, whereas most nationalists and Republicans came from a Catholic one. Subsequently, this would garner a response from the Vatican to the 1981 hunger strike.

On the 28th of April 1981, Monsignor John Magee, envoy to Pope John Paul II, would visit Long Kesh in a bid to persuade the hunger strikers to call off their protest.[73] The year previously, the Pontiff had personally written to Margaret Thatcher to outline his concerns regarding the treatment of Republican prisoners amidst the 1980 hunger strike.[74] Whilst on the visit, Monsignor Magee would present the hunger strikers with ten gold crucifixes, personally blessed by Pope John Paul II, in order to provide them with comfort throughout their ordeal.

All hunger strikers would subsequently be buried with their gifted crucifix, with the exception of Patsy O'Hara, who passed it on as a gift to his mother Peggy instead.[75]

Following her death in 2015, the O'Hara family would pass the crucifix onto James Connolly House,[76] the museum of the Irish Republican Socialist Movement located in Derry, where it remains on display to this day, serving as another reminder of the international impact of the 1981 hunger strike.

Canada

Returning to the Americas, Canada also held notable displays of solidarity with the hunger strikers of 1981. Again, like its southern neighbour, the United States, a key factor in this was the significant percentage of the Canadian population that could claim Irish heritage.

Following the devastation of *An Gorta Mór* in the 1840s, and the forced exile of upwards of one million Irish people from their homeland, many would take the long journey across the Atlantic to not just the US, but also to its larger northern neighbour.

Establishing Irish communities in the same manner as in Australia, Britain and the US, Irish-Canadians would also provide financial and logistical support to Republicans when conflict broke out in 1969. Though not as extensive as its US counterpart, a NORAID-style fundraising and gun-running operation would be established in Toronto that year,[77] when a number of Republican sympathisers in the city organised for funds and mining detonators[78] to be sent to Ireland in order to aid the fledgling Provisional IRA.

Just over a decade later, this Irish-Canadian solidarity would continue at the outset of the Irish hunger strike. However, as many Canadians of Irish descent had also come from an Ulster unionist background, it did not always pass without incident.

On the 25th of April, when tensions surrounding the hunger strike were beginning to reach their peak, the Irish Prisoner of War Committee, a group set up to raise awareness[79] of the strike amongst the Canadian public, held a demonstration outside the British Airways office in Toronto.[80] Tense scenes would follow when British-sympathising unionists held a counter-demonstration in response, with police separating the two groups. Canadian state broadcaster CBC was present on the day, interviewing attendees of both events.

The attempt at intimidation by unionists would not succeed however, and in July, at which stage six hunger strikers had died, Canadian supporters of the strike would score their biggest coup.

First held in 1975 in France, the Group of Six (G6) sought to bring together the world's richest industrialised nations - at the time, France, the US, Britain, West Germany, Japan and Italy - in a forum setting. One year later at its US summit, Canada would officially join, giving the group its more well-known name, the G7. A yearly meeting would be held in each member nation, with Canada's turn coming in 1981.

On the 20th of July 1981, a week after the death of Martin Hurson, the G7 leaders, among them Margaret Thatcher, would meet in Montebello, Quebec for the group's seventh annual summit. With the eyes of the world's media on the Canadian province, more than 200 Republican sympathisers would gather at the summit to protest against the presence of Thatcher,[81] and to highlight the ongoing situation back in Ireland, their message going global as a result. Just like the similar solidarity events held in the neighbouring US, it would once again show the impact that the 1981 hunger had had across the Atlantic.

Cuba

A former Spanish colony from the late 15th century until Madrid's defeat in the 1898 Spanish-American war, the first half-century of Cuba's independence would see Havana consolidate its ties[82] with the US, who had intervened militarily[83] in the Cuban War of Independence following the sinking of the USS *Maine*, a US Navy ship despatched to Havana Harbour in order to protect US sugarcane interests during the uprising against Spanish rule on the island nation. In 1952, this consolidation of ties would culminate in former president Fulgencio Batista seizing power in a military coup, one that would be quickly recognised by Washington, who offered its full support to the new regime.

Batista's rule would not prove popular with ordinary Cubans however, and discontent would quickly grow in the Caribbean nation at the increasing privatisation of Cuba's lucrative sugar industry by US interests, Batista's ties to US organised crime syndicates, and the growing gap between rich and poor. On the 26th of July 1953, this unrest would ultimately lead to attorney-turned-revolutionary Fidel Castro, a candidate in the Cuban election that had been cancelled as a result of Batista's coup, leading an armed attack on the Moncada Barracks in the city of Santiago de Cuba. Captured by government forces shortly afterwards, Castro and his brother Raúl would be sentenced to 15 and 13 years respectively for their roles in the attack, in which many of the rebels who took part had been killed or executed in the aftermath.

After two years however, the Batista government would bow to pressure from an increasingly hostile Cuban public and release Castro and his fellow rebels, having no longer regarded them as a security threat. This would ultimately prove to be a costly mistake.

Relocating to Mexico upon his release in 1955, where he would meet Argentinian revolutionary Che Guevara, Castro would re-organise his rebels as the 26th of July Movement, in honour of the date of the attack on Moncada. The following November, he set sail on the ship *Granma* towards Cuba, once again with the intention of overthrowing Batista's rule.

Landing in Cuba in early December 1956, a two-year guerrilla campaign would begin against government forces, eventually resulting in a victory for the rebels on New Year's Day 1959, when Batista would flee in exile to the Dominican Republic. Following centuries of Spanish colonial rule, and decades of overt US influence, the new Socialist government of Fidel Castro would adopt a markedly anti-Western stance, which, at the height of Cold War tensions between NATO and the Soviet Union, would immediately place it in Washington's crosshairs.

In 1960, Washington would impose a stringent trade embargo on Cuba, one that remains in place to this day. A year later, CIA-trained Cuban exiles would land at the country's southwestern Bay of Pigs in an attempt to overthrow Castro. In a significant foreign policy blunder for the United States, they would be defeated by Cuban Forces within three days, leading to ongoing tensions that would culminate in the October 1962 Cuban Missile Crisis, when in response to US nuclear missiles being placed in Italy and Turkey, intended to strike the Soviet Union, Moscow would respond in kind by placing its own missiles in Cuba, ninety miles from the Florida coast. The ensuing US Naval blockade of the island is regarded as the closest the world has ever been to a nuclear war, ending only when both sides respectively agreed to remove their missiles from the offending locations.

The anti-Western sentiment of Cuba would continue however, and by 1981 this would grow to a show of solidarity with the hunger strikers of Ireland, with Margaret Thatcher being a key ally of US President Ronald Reagan, who had assumed office the previous year and had pursued a foreign policy based on the containment of socialism in Latin America.

On the 15h of September 1981, the Inter-Parliamentary Union, an international organisation of national parliaments, held its 68th annual conference in Havana. Addressing the audience in a lengthy speech that denounced the actions of the US and Israel in Latin America and the Middle East, Fidel Castro then brought attention to the situation in the north of Ireland.

Referring to *"Irish patriots"* who were *"writing one of the most heroic chapters in the history of mankind"*, Castro lamented that *"Mankind should feel ashamed that this terrible crime is being committed before its very eyes".* Going on to condemn the *"stubbornness, intransigence, cruelty, and insensitivity of the British Government"* the Cuban president would finish by declaring *"Let tyrants tremble before men capable of dying for their ideals after 60 days on hunger strike!"* becoming one of the few world leaders who would voice their support for the hunger strikers.

Indeed, two decades later, in December 2001, a monument would be unveiled[84] in Havana's Parque Victor Hugo to commemorate the ten Republicans who had died. A lasting reminder of the enduring impact that the 1981 hunger had had on the island nation.

Palestine

In the late 19th century, a wave of Jewish immigration from Eastern Europe to Palestine, then part of the Ottoman Empire, would coincide with the rise of the political ideology known as Zionism, which envisaged the establishment of a Jewish state in the Middle East.

The first *Aliyah* (Hebrew for "Ascent") would take place from 1881 until 1903, with the Zionist lobby being officially established in 1897, when Theodor Herzl founded the World Zionist Organisation (WZO) in Basel, Switzerland. The second wave of Jewish immigration, this time coming mainly from Russia, would begin in 1904, lasting for a decade until 1914, when the first World War began.

It would be during this period that the influence of Zionism would be rubber stamped.

In 1916, with Britain on the verge of a catastrophic military defeat to Germany, the British Zionist lobby approached Downing Street with an offer. In return for instructing their American counterparts to lobby for the United States, then a neutral party, to enter the war, Britain would assist in the establishment of a Jewish state in Palestine,[85] with the Ottomans being on the opposing side to London at the time.

Taking the Zionists up on their offer, the US would subsequently enter the conflict in April 1917, turning the tide significantly in Britain and the Allied Powers' favour. In November that year, Arthur Balfour, former Prime Minister of the UK and then-Foreign Secretary to the government of David Lloyd George, would issue the Balfour Declaration, which

41

reiterated Britain's support to Lord Rothschild, scion of the famed banking dynasty and a leading member of Britain's Jewish community, that Downing Street would assist in the establishment of a Jewish state in Palestine.

Following the subsequent defeat of the Central Powers the following year, the Ottoman Empire, already in decline at the beginning of the conflict, would see its territories rapidly diminish. In 1916, following the initial Zionist approach to Downing Street, Britain and France, then allies in the Triple Entente, signed the Sykes-Picot Agreement, named after both countries' respective chief negotiators, in order to determine London and Paris' envisaged spheres of influence in Ottoman territories post-victory. In 1920, Palestine would become a British mandate.

In the decade that followed, large-scale Jewish immigration to Palestine would continue, again coming mainly from Eastern Europe and Russia. By the 1930s, Jewish immigration to Palestine was on such a scale that tensions had begun to arise with the native Arab population. Tensions that would soon erupt.

In 1933, following the appointment of Adolf Hitler as Chancellor of Germany, Berlin would sign the Haavara Agreement with the Zionist Federation of Germany, which would see Jews in Germany being granted free passage to emigrate to Palestine, provided they first sold their German assets, before being reimbursed upon arrival in Palestine by the Anglo-Palestine Bank, which had also taken part in the deal under the direction of the Jewish Agency for Israel, a branch of the World Zionist Organisation established specifically to encourage Jewish emigration to Palestine.

With the Haavara Agreement exacerbating already existing tensions in Palestine, riots would break out in Jerusalem in October 1933[86] following the breakup by British police of a planned demonstration by the Arab Executive Committee. Violence would also break out in the cities of Jaffa, Haifa and Nablus in the weeks that followed, leading to dozens of deaths and injuries.

The 1933 riots would not prove to be an isolated incident however, and just three years later in 1936, a large-scale revolt would break out in Palestine against British rule and the scale of Jewish immigration, lasting until 1939 and the outbreak of World War II.

It would be the aftermath of this conflict that would have the most serious repercussions for the Palestinians.

Following the Allied victory in Europe, Palestine would once again find itself beset by instability, this time including attacks on British Forces by Zionist paramilitaries. In July 1946, the Zionist group Irgun bombed Jerusalem's King David Hotel, headquarters of the British administration, killing 91 people. The following year, in response to the execution of three of its members, Irgun would kidnap and hang two British sergeants. Having booby-trapped the bodies with explosives, another officer would be injured when attempting to retrieve them, leading to widespread revulsion in Britain. Downing Street would soon decide that its presence in the region was no longer tenable.

Approaching the newly formed United Nations to help resolve the issue, a plan was put in place to partition Palestine into Arab and Jewish states,[87] with Jews receiving the majority of the land despite being an overall minority in Palestine.[88] An unworkable plan, and one that would soon lead to conflict.

43

H-BLOCK INTERNATIONAL

On the 15th of May 1948, in an event known in the Arab world as the *Nakba* ("catastrophe"), 700,000[89] Palestinians would become refugees overnight with the formation of the state of Israel, whose newly-established forces would begin an ethnic cleansing campaign against the indigenous Arab population. A war would immediately begin with the surrounding Arab states, ending in an armistice agreement in which Egypt gained control of the coastal Gaza Strip and Jordan gained control of the West Bank of the Jordan River.

The vast majority of Palestine would remain under Israeli occupation however, and both Gaza and the West Bank would subsequently be annexed by Tel Aviv in 1967, following a conflict between Israel and an Arab coalition led by Egypt, Jordan and Syria.

This occupation, the ethnic cleansing of an indigenous population to make way for foreign settlers, and Britain's central role in the situation, would bear a stark similarity to the history of Ireland, in particular the Cromwellian conquests and plantation of Ulster. As such, despite their geographical distance, a natural affinity would begin to develop between Ireland and Palestine.

In the 1970s, following the outbreak of violence in Ireland and the emergence of the IRA and INLA, both groups would develop links with the militant Palestine Liberation Organisation (PLO), organising arms deals and for members of both groups to attend training camps in friendly countries such as Lebanon and Libya.

As the 1980s dawned and Republicans began hunger strikes in order to be recognised as political prisoners, this relationship would lead to a striking display of solidarity from Palestine with the hunger strikers of 1981.

In July that year, at which stage six hunger strikers had died, Palestinian prisoners in the Nafha desert prison wrote a letter of solidarity[90] for the remaining strikers, which was then smuggled out and sent to Ireland.

Beginning by addressing the *"the families of the martyrs oppressed by the British ruling class"* and *"the families of Bobby Sands and his martyred comrades"*, the letter then expressed *"salutes and solidarity"* with Irish Republicans in their *"confrontation against the oppressive terrorist rule enforced upon the Irish people by the British ruling elite"*. Saluting the *"heroic struggle of Bobby Sands and his comrades"*, the letter declared that they had *"sacrificed the most valuable possession of any human being. They gave their lives for freedom."*. Then going on to outline the conditions that they and the Palestinian people faced, and their own struggle for freedom, they would finish by once again reiterating their support for the Irish hunger strikers, declaring *"we support your struggle and cause of freedom against English domination, against Zionism and against fascism in the world."*, once again illustrating the impact that the hunger strike had had worldwide, this time in the Middle East.

Iran

At the turn of the 20th century, following a report by French geologist Jacques de Morgan that the discovery of petroleum seepages in southwestern Iran (then Persia) indicated the presence of commercially profitable oil reserves in the vast mountainous country, the interest of British business tycoon William Knox D'arcy was piqued. In 1901, he signed an agreement with Iranian monarch, Shah Mozaffar ad-Din, allowing him to prospect for oil throughout Iran. An arrangement that was highly favourable towards the British businessman, the D'arcy Concession granted him permission to direct expeditions throughout vast swathes of Iran, and the majority of any potential profit.

Initially unsuccessful in the first few years, and having to sell his shares in the expedition to the Glasgow-based Burmah Oil as a result, D'arcy's fortunes would change in 1908 with the discovery of oil in the city of Masjed Soleyman. In line with the conditions set out in the D'arcy Concession, Burmah Oil would establish the Anglo-Persian Oil Company (APOC) in 1909 with D'arcy as director. With Downing Street having decided in the same time period that oil would replace coal as the main energy source for its naval fleet, and having encouraged D'arcy's decision to sell his shares to Burmah Oil for fear of losing out on any potential oil discovery to France or Russia, the British government would become majority shareholder of APOC in 1914. Subsequently, Iran would go on to become a key strategic asset to British interests in the decades that followed.

Indeed, this strategic importance would be illustrated during the second World War, when following Germany's invasion of the Soviet Union in 1941, both Moscow and London would organise a joint-invasion of Iran in order to curtail German influence in the region, and to protect each country's respective interests in Iran. In the Soviet Union's case, this would be the Allied supply lines from Europe, and in Britain's, the Abadan oil refinery in the southwestern Khuzestan region. Following the end of the conflict, British troops would remain in Iran until 1946.

It would be in the years following the end of World War II however, that discontent would begin to emerge amongst the Iranian public at Britain's relationship with Iran, with many seeing it as an unbalanced relationship that favoured London over Tehran. This wave of discontent would coincide with the rise of the National Front, established by Iranian nationalist Mohammad Mosaddegh in 1949, which called for Iran's lucrative oil industry to be nationalised. A move that would take place two years later in 1951, with Mosaddegh becoming Prime Minister shortly afterwards.

Britain, having already lost its superpower status since the end of World War II, and fearing that Iran would now gravitate towards the neighbouring Soviet Union amidst the beginnings of Cold War tensions, did not take kindly to the establishment of the National Iranian Oil Company. In response, the Labour government of Clement Atlee would impose a Cuba-style economic blockade against Iran, which would go as far as deploying British warships to the Persian Gulf, a short distance from the Abadan refinery. The subsequent elections of Winston Churchill as British Prime Minister in late 1951, and Dwight D. Eisenhower as US President in 1952, would exacerbate matters further.

In August 1953, the intelligence services of both countries, MI6 and the CIA, fomented an uprising against Mosaddegh's rule. Known to the British by the codename Operation Boot, and to the US as Operation Ajax, this coup would involve the widespread dissemination of anti-Mosaddegh propaganda, and the organising of violent protests that would soon sweep Iran. Culminating in the overthrow and imprisonment of Mosaddegh, who would spend the remainder of his life under house arrest until his death in 1967, the coup would see Iranian General Fazlollah Zahedi installed as Prime Minister, and the consolidation of power of the pro–Western head of state, Shah Reza Pahlavi, who would soon seek to rubber stamp his authority.

In 1954, the Shah signed the Consortium Agreement, allowing Western oil conglomerates 40% ownership of Iran's oil and refinery infrastructure. APOC, renamed as the Anglo-Iranian Oil Company in 1935 and sidelined during Mosaddegh's nationalisation period, would be re-established as British Petroleum as a result. In 1957, Pahlavi established the Bureau for Intelligence and Security of the State, more commonly known as SAVAK, a secret police force intended to monitor Iranians opposed to his rule, and to prevent another Mosaddegh-type figure coming to power.

Indeed, the feelings of discontent that had brought Mosaddegh to power were still widespread in Iran, with many seeing the country as being reduced to a mere vassal-state, beholden to foreign interests in an arrangement that benefited the ruling elite at the cost of ordinary Iranians. As the 1960s dawned, and the Shah began an extensive modernisation policy known as the White Revolution, his rule would soon also begin to draw the ire of Iran's Islamic clergy, who regarded the reforms as a form of Westernisation of the predominantly Shia Muslim country. Most prominent amongst these religious dissidents was Ayatollah Ruhollah Khomeini.

In 1964, following Khomeini's vocal condemnation of the Shah's reforms, Pahlavi would respond by exiling the Ayatollah to Turkey. A move that if anything, would increase the Ayatollah's popularity amongst traditional Muslims in Iran even further. Indeed, one year later, reformist Prime Minister, Hassan Ali Mansur, would be assassinated by Shia Islamist group Fadayan-e Islam, illustrating the extent of Islamic opposition to the Shah's secular policies.

As the 1960s progressed and the 1970s dawned, widespread discontent with the Shah's rule would continue to grow. In 1971, a state ceremony in Persepolis to mark 2,500 years of the Persian Empire drew widespread condemnation from Iranians, due to the consumption of alcohol by foreign dignitaries at the event, and the opulent splendour on display being in stark contrast to the poverty of surrounding rural regions. In 1975, opposition parties were banned in Iran, and in 1976, the country's official calendar was changed from the traditional Islamic Hijri format to one coinciding with the ascension to the throne of Cyrus the Great, a move that once again incensed Iran's Muslims. The stage would soon be set for the Shah's removal from power.

In January 1978, following the publication of a disparaging letter about the Ayatollah in one of Iran's most widely circulated newspapers, thousands of Iranians took to the streets in the city of Qom - considered a holy site in Shia Islam - in opposition to the Shah's rule. Several days of protest would ultimately end with government forces opening fire on demonstrators, leading to a number of deaths, and setting in motion a chain of events that would lead to dramatic geopolitical upheaval for both Iran and the entire Middle East.

One month later, following a memorial ceremony for the victims of the shootings in the city of Tabriz, violence would once again break out between protesters and government forces, a pattern that would soon spread throughout the entirety of Iran. In September, following the introduction of martial law, Pahlavi's forces would open fire on demonstrators in Tehran, leading to dozens of deaths in an event known as Black Friday. In response, strikes would be declared throughout Iran, including the oil sector in particular. The Shah's rule was quickly becoming untenable.

In early 1979, following a meeting in Guadeloupe, between the US, Britain, France and West Germany, that came to the conclusion that there was no feasible way of restoring stability in Iran while the Shah remained in power, Pahlavi's fate was sealed. On the 16th of January, nine days after the Guadeloupe Conference, Pahlavi would flee Iran in exile, bringing to an end more than two and a half millennia of Persian and Iranian monarchical rule. Khomeini would return to Iran shortly afterwards after a decade and a half in exile, establishing the Islamic Republic. A state that, in stark contrast to its predecessor, would adopt a markedly anti-Western stance.

Indeed, with Britain having played a key role in the propping up of the Shah's rule and the consolidation of ties with the West, this stance would be illustrated during the hunger strike in the north of Ireland, just over two years later.

Following the death of Bobby Sands, the Iranian Ambassador to Sweden, Abdul Rahim Govahi, would be despatched to Belfast to serve as Tehran's official representative at the funeral,[91] with Iran joining Cuba as the one of the few governments to publicly express their official condolences upon Sands' death. An official plaque would be presented to Bobby Sands' mother on behalf of the people of Iran also.[92]

This would not be the only response from the Iranian government to the 1981 Irish hunger strike, as a street in Tehran would also be named after Bobby Sands upon his death. However, this was no ordinary street. The previously named Winston Churchill Street was home to Iran's British Embassy, meaning that all official correspondence coming to and from the building would have to bear the name of the young IRA Volunteer from Belfast as a result. To avoid the embarrassment of this situation, the Embassy would have to change its mailing address to a side entrance on nearby Ferdowsi Street. Once again, the impact of the Irish hunger strike had been felt across the globe.

Aftermath of the Hunger Strike

Following the death of Michael Devine in August 1981, six other Republican prisoners remained on hunger strike. In the weeks that followed however, three IRA prisoners, having begun to lapse into comas, were taken off the strike following outside intervention by their families, with another, INLA prisoner Liam McCloskey, willingly ending his involvement when his family made it clear that they too would seek medical treatment had he began to lose consciousness. Though a number of other prisoners would begin to refuse food in late August and throughout September, the hunger strike would officially be declared over on the 3rd of October 1981. Three days later, recently appointed Secretary of State Jim Prior would effectively grant the majority of the prisoners' demands (the final one, the right to not do prison work, would be restored two years later following the destruction of prison workshops during rioting). Political status, removed in 1976, had effectively been restored to Republican prisoners.

The lasting impact of the 1981 hunger strike however, would be the political trajectory it would send militant Republicanism on. On the 9th of April, one month after beginning the hunger strike, Bobby Sands would be elected as an MP on the traditional Republican basis of abstaining from taking seats in Stormont or Westminster. A massive propaganda coup for Republicans, Sands' election would result in Britain passing the Representation of the People Act, which forbade anyone serving a prison sentence of more than one year from standing in a British election. The impact of Sands' electoral victory however, would go on to play a hugely influential role on Republicanism.

At that year's Sinn Féin *Ard Fheis* ("high assembly", the annual party conference), held less than a month after the end of the hunger strike, the strategy of the armalite and the ballot box was put forward, in which Republicanism would seek electoral victory in the north of Ireland on an abstentionist basis, while at the same time waging a military campaign against the British occupation. Though ostensibly portrayed as a strategy that assigned equal importance to both the military and political campaign, it would soon become apparent that the latter was to be given precedence.

At the same Ard Fheis, the decision would be taken that Sinn Féin would drop its longstanding *Éire Nua* (New Ireland) policy. A comprehensive document outlining the Republican administration of an Ireland post-British withdrawal, Éire Nua envisaged a decentralised federal model based on Ireland's four provinces, Leinster, Munster, Connacht and Ulster. The 1981 Ard Fheis also marked the sidelining of Sinn Féin President and Vice President, Ruairí Ó Brádaigh and Dáithí Ó Conaill, authors of the Éire Nua document and two of the main architects behind the reorganisation of the IRA following the 1969 split, and the emergence of a faction led by Gerry Adams and Martin McGuinness.

Indeed, both Ó Brádaigh and Ó Conaill would resign from their leadership positions following the dropping of Éire Nua, and would be replaced by Adams and McGuinness in 1983, who continued to direct Republicanism on an incrementally reformist path. This would culminate in the decision to recognise the southern Leinster House parliament at the 1986 Ard Fheis, and take seats if elected. This would provoke fierce opposition from Ó Brádaigh, who gave an almost prophetic speech at the event, predicting that entering Leinster House would subsequently lead to entering Stormont, resulting in a political settlement in the north of Ireland, wherein a local government, composed of both nationalists and unionists, would administer British rule on behalf of Westminster. A situation that would become a reality in the decades that followed.

Despite Ó Brádaigh's protests, the motion to recognise Leinster House would pass. In response, Ó Brádaigh and Ó Conaill staged a walkout and subsequently re-organised Sinn Féin as *Republican Sinn Féin*, with the decision to enter Leinster House being prohibited by the Sinn Féin constitution, which forbade the promotion of such a move, effectively expelling the Adams-led faction. The IRA would be reorganised as the Continuity IRA in a similar fashion. It must be noted however, that in Irish political discourse, the term "Sinn Féin" is generally associated with the larger Provisional Sinn Féin faction that was established in 1986, and whose armed wing would continue its military campaign for another eleven years before declaring a permanent ceasefire in 1997.

In 1998, Provisional Sinn Féin signed the Good Friday Agreement, which much like the Anglo-Irish agreement of 1922, would effectively act as a surrender to Britain by legitimising London's claim to the six north-eastern counties. Entering the newly re-established Stormont parliament shortly afterwards, where they would administer British rule in the north of Ireland alongside unionists, Ruairí Ó Brádaigh's predictions from twelve years previously had ultimately come to pass. In 2005, the Provisional IRA would officially decommission their vast arsenal of weaponry.

Republican Sinn Féin however, or *Sinn Féin Poblachtach* to give the organisation its Irish name, would re-adopt the Éire Nua policy upon its reorganisation in 1986, and continues to promote it to this day.

Originally published in 1971, Éire Nua envisaged the nationalisation of Ireland's vast natural resources and non-alignment with the two main power blocs of the time, namely NATO and the Warsaw Pact. It also opposed entry into the European Economic Community, which both Ireland and Britain subsequently became members of in 1973. The event of Éire Nua becoming a reality however, would be a geopolitically precarious one.

Ireland, located at the edge of westernmost Europe, with the United States directly across the Atlantic, would run the serious risk of becoming politically isolated should it withdraw from the power structures of the Collective West, namely the European Union and the multinational corporations that possess a significant stake in Irish natural resources. The likelihood of a coup or colour revolution, fomented by Western intelligence agencies, would be strong. As would the possibility of it escalating into a Yugoslavia or Libya-style military intervention, with the intention of re-installing a government in Ireland more agreeable to international corporate interests.

The authors of Éire Nua were prescient of such possibilities however, and had made preparations for such events.

A key aspect of the document would be to seek membership of the Non-Aligned Movement and to develop trade links with other smaller neutral countries in Europe, and countries in Africa, Asia and Latin America that shared a similar anti-imperialist ethos. A concept as relevant in Cold War 1971 as it is in the 21st century with the emergence of the multipolar world

Following the end of the Cold War and the dissolution of the Soviet Union in 1991, the United States would emerge as the world's sole political, economic and military superpower. The previous arrangement in international relations, in which the US and USSR maintained bipolar parity in the aforementioned fields, would be replaced with a new geopolitical reality where Washington held unipolar influence on world affairs.

Following the turn of the 21st century and a series of costly military misadventures following the 9/11 attacks however, a new arrangement in international relations would begin to emerge. In 2009, Brazil, Russia, India and China would hold a summit in the Russian city of Yekaterinburg, intended to explore mutually-beneficial investment opportunities. Joining them at the following year's meeting in Brazil would be South Africa, leading to the name BRICS for the now-highly influential international body, which has now seen Iran, Egypt, Ethiopia and the United Arab Emirates go on to become members. In 2013, China launched the Belt and Road Initiative (BRI), a global infrastructure development programme intended to be run on a mutually beneficial basis between Beijing and member nations, and in 2015, Russia intervened militarily in Syria at the request of the government of Bashar al-Assad, whose leadership had been threatened by regime-change from the West, the dominant military influence in the West Asia region prior to the Russian operation. New global power blocs had established themselves outside the Collective West's traditional powerbase of the US and Western Europe.

Blocs that, for a newly-unified Ireland that had just exited the power structures of the Collective West yet remained within its existing geographical boundaries, would prove to be ideal political and trading partners. A move that would once again continue the long-standing Republican tradition of fostering international ties with like-minded allies, just as had been seen in the hunger strike of 1981.

Notes

The Hunger Strikers

1. Denis O'Hearn *Bobby Sands - Nothing but an Unfinished Song* 2006 p.3
2. David Beresford *Ten Men Dead* 1987 p.58
3. Account of Bernadette Sands, sister of Bobby.
4. Ibid.
5. David Beresford *Ten Men Dead* 1987 p.151
6. David Beresford *Ten Men Dead* 1987 p.152
7. David Beresford *Ten Men Dead* 1987 p.157
8. *Irish Republican News* Francis Hughes and Raymond McCreesh 26th of October 2011.
9. David Beresford *Ten Men Dead* 1987 p.199
10. Henry McDonald & Jack Holland *I.N.L.A. Deadly Divisions* 2010 p.213
11. David Beresford *Ten Men Dead* 1987 p.208
12. Ibid.
13. Ibid.
14. Ibid
15. Ibid.
16. David Beresford *Ten Men Dead* 1987 p.280
17. Ibid.

18. David Beresford *Ten Men Dead* 1987 p.286

19. Prison communication between Martin Hurson and Sinn Féin official.

20. David Beresford *Ten Men Dead* 1987 p.315

21. Prison communication between Martin Hurson and Sinn Féin official.

22. Prison communication between Kevin Lynch and Sinn Féin official.

23. Ibid.

24. David Beresford *Ten Men Dead* 1987 p.229

25. Prison communication between Kieran Doherty and Sinn Féin official.

26. Ibid.

27. Ibid.

28. David Beresford *Ten Men Dead* 1987 p.366

29. Ibid.

30. *Bobby Sands Trust* Kieran Doherty

31. David Beresford *Ten Men Dead* 1987 p.242

32. David Beresford *Ten Men Dead* 1987 p.244

33. David Beresford *Ten Men Dead* 1987 p.397

34. David Beresford *Ten Men Dead* 1987 p.399

35. David Beresford *Ten Men Dead* 1987 p.401-402

36. Ibid.

Britain

37. *The Irish Crisis* Charles Trevelyan 1848.

38. 1841 census of Ireland, which recorded the highest-ever population of 8.2 million.

39. Ibid.

40. *An Phoblacht* The impact of the hunger strike in Britain Joe Dwyer 20th of May 2021.

41. Ibid.

42. Ibid.

43. Ibid.

44. Ibid.

45. Ibid.

United States

46. *The Guardian* Ex-gunrunner fights ban on rebel Sinn Fein (sic) Henry McDonald 18th of July 2004.

47. *The New York Times* 5 ARE ACQUITTED IN BROOKLYN OF PLOT TO RUN GUNS TO THE I.R.A Robert D. McFadden 6th of November 1982.

48. *The Burkean* Hunger Striker's American Legacy Martin Galvin 2021.

49. *United Press International* 27th of November 1980.

50. *United Press International* 5th of May 1981.

51. *The Irish Times* Bernie Sanders wrote to Thatcher on hunger strikers 19th of February 2016.

52. *BBC* Nine O'Clock News 5th of May 1981.

53. David Beresford *Ten Men Dead* 1987 p.131

54. Ibid.

55. *United Press International* Irish-Americans boycott British Michelle Mundth 7th of May 1981.

56. *United Press International* Americans mourn Sands' death: tell British to get out Michelle Mundth 5th of May 1981.

57. *The Burkean* Hunger Striker's American Legacy Martin Galvin 2021.

58. *The New York Times* PRINCE CHARLES PAY A QUICK VISIT TO CITY Fred Ferretti 18th of June 1981.

59. *The Burkean* Hunger Striker's American Legacy Martin Galvin 2021.

60. *The New York Times* ON THIRD AVE., 1,500 RALLY OVER DEATH OF SANDS William G. Blair 6th of May 1981.

61. *United Press International* Irish-Americans boycott British Michelle Mundth 7th of May 1981.

Australia

62. *An Phoblacht* Support from afar - Australian support for the hunger strikers Chris Raleigh 7th of June 2001.

63. Ibid.

64. Ibid.

65. Ibid.

66. *An Phoblacht* Support from afar - Australian support for the hunger strikers Chris Raleigh 7th of June 2001.

67. *Green Left* Irish hunger strike remembered Emma Clancy 18th of May 2007.

68. *An Phoblacht* Support from afar - Australian support for the hunger strikers Chris Raleigh 7th of June 2001.

69. *Belfast Live* Street in Australia named after hunger striker Bobby Sands Sheila McStravick 26th of February 2015.

France

70. David Beresford *Ten Men Dead* 1987 p.132

71. Ibid.

72. *France 24* 'Street warfare in Paris: Thatcher vs Sands' 12th of April 2013.

Vatican City

73. *BBC* Nine O'Clock News 28th of April 1981.

74. *Belfast Telegraph* Pope John Paul II had hunger strikers concern 29th of December 2010.

75. *IRSP official website* The story behind the 1981 Hunger Striker's Crucifix 8th of August 2019.

76. Ibid.

Canada

77. *Wikipedia* Provisional Irish Republican Army arms importation.

78. *Ibid.*

79. *The Hamilton Spectator* Obituary for Michael Quigley 11th of March 2024.

80. *CBC* news report, 25th of April 1981.

81. *CBC* Reporters, protesters, and the history of the G7 20th of July 1981.

Cuba

82. *Platt Amendment to the 1901 Army Appropriations Bill* US Congress, 2nd of March 1901.

83. *Joint Resolution For the recognition of the independence of the people of Cuba, demanding that the Government of Spain relinquish its authority and government in the Island of Cuba, and to withdraw its land and naval forces from Cuba and Cuban waters, and directing the President of the United States to use the land and naval forces of the United States to carry these resolutions into effect* US Congress, 20th of April 1898.

84. *The Irish Times* Adams unveils Bobby Sands memorial in Cuba 18th of December 2001.

Palestine

85. Speech by prominent US-Jewish businessman and vocal anti-Zionist Benjamin H. Freedman at the Willard Hotel, Washington, 1961.

86. *The Sunday Times* Riots in Palestine 29th of October 1933.

87. Resolution 181 (II) - United Nations Partition Plan for Palestine, 29th of November 1947.

88. United Nations Special Committee on Palestine report, 3rd of September 1947.

89. United Nations Relief and Works Agency for Palestine Refugees in the Near East.

90. *The Starry Plough* September 1981.

Iran

91. David Beresford *Ten Men Dead* 1987 p.132

92. *Bobby Sands Trust* The Night We Named Bobby Sands Street Pedram Moallemian.

Bibliography

Afterlives Richard O'Rawe 2011

Ten Men Dead David Beresford 1987

I.N.L.A. - Deadly Divisions Henry McDonald & Jack Holland 2010

Bobby Sands - Nothing but an Unfinished Song Denis O'Hearn 2006

Printed in Great Britain
by Amazon